Do bugs have Bottoms?

and other extremely important questions (and answers) from the Science Museum

Glenn Murphy

Illustrated by Mike Phillips

MACMILLAN CHILDREN'S BOOKS

First published 2011 by Macmillan Children's Books
a division of Macmillan Publishers Limited
20 New Wharf Road, London N1 9RR
Basingstoke and Oxford
Associated companies throughout the world
www.panmacmillan.com

ISBN 978-0-956-62767-4

1 3 5 7 9 8 6 4 2

A CIP catalogue record for this book is available from the British Library.

Printed and bound in Great Britain by CPI Bookmarque, Croydon CR0 4TD

The text paper within this book was donated by Abitibi Consolidated and
Paper Management Services Ltd

The paper and board used in this paperback by Hodder Children's Books
and Macmillan Children's Books are natural recyclable products made from
wood grown in sustainable forests. The manufacturing processes conform
to the environmental regulations of the country of origin.

Do bugs have Bottoms?

Glenn Murphy received his masters in science communication from London's Imperial College of Science, Technology and Medicine. He wrote his first popular science book, *Why Is Snot Green?*, while working at the Science Museum in London. In 2007 he moved to the United States. He now lives and works in Raleigh, North Carolina, with his wife, Heather, and an increasingly large and ill-tempered cat.

Why Is Snot Green? was shortlisted for the Blue Peter Book Awards 2007, Best Book with Facts category, and the Royal Society Prize for Science Books Junior Prize 2008.

Also by Glenn Murphy

Why Is Snot Green?
and other extremely important questions
(and answers) from the Science Museum

How Loud Can You Burp?
and other extremely important questions
(and answers) from the Science Museum

Stuff That Scares Your Pants Off!
The Science Museum Book of Scary Things
(and how to avoid them)

Science: Sorted! Space, Black Holes and Stuff

Science: Sorted! Evolution, Nature and Stuff

This book has been specially written and published for World Book Day 2011. For further information please see www.worldbookday.com

World Book Day in the UK and Ireland is made possible by generous sponsorship from National Book Tokens, participating publishers, authors and booksellers. Booksellers who accept the £1 World Book Day Token bear the full cost of redeeming it.

Contents

Many thanks to

Mike Phillips, for continued illustrations
of his brilliance

Gaby Morgan and all at
Macmillan Children's Books

Deborah Bloxam-Patterson at the
Science Museum, London

Prof Alun Williams BVMS, PhD, DipECVP,
MRCVS, FHEA Chair of Veterinary Diagnostic
Pathology Department of Veterinary Medicine,
University of Cambridge

Harsimran Sekhon of the Slough
Grammar School, UK – aspiring writer and
dedicated GlennMurphyBooks fan!

Justin, Serena and Matthew Sudbury

The Murphs and the Witts

And all our friends, far and wide

Why do sweaty feet stink?

Actually, sweaty feet don't stink at all. It's the sweat-eating bacteria that live on them that smell so bad. That delightful, distinctive odour of cheesy feet is released from bugs left to grow inside your stinky socks and shoes.

Sweat-eating bacteria that live on your feet?! *Gross!*

Believe me, it gets worse. These sweat-eating bugs aren't confined to your feet. They're all over your body. The average adult has a total skin area of around 2 square metres. And upon that skin live over 1,000 species of bacteria, from up to twenty different biological families (or rather, *phyla*).

That's the most disgusting thing I've ever heard. Tell me more. What are they *doing* there?

For the most part, they're just hanging out – eating and drinking the sweat, skin oil, dead skin cells and other wastes that build up on the surface of your body. It's like one big bacterial party.

Isn't that dangerous? I mean, don't bacteria give you diseases?

Some of them do, yes. But most of the 'bug'

species that commonly live on human skin – such *corynebacteria*, *micrococci* and *staphylococci* – are pretty harmless. And even the ones that can do us harm are kept safely at bay by the solid fleshy barrier of the skin itself. Once in a while, though, they can (quite literally) get under your skin and cause problems. If you suffer a nasty cut, graze or burn, bacteria can slip in through the break in your skin's defences and form a bacterial invasion (or *infection*).

. . . and then you have to take antibiotics, right?

Well, even when this invasion does happen, your immune cells usually fight the bugs off. It's only when the immune cells fail – and the infection threatens to hang around, or spread to your bloodstream – that doctors have to attack them with antibiotic drugs. And in fact, antibiotics don't typically kill the bacteria either. They just stop them growing or feeding for a while, which gives the body's own immune cells a chance to call for reinforcements and mount a counter-attack.

So if all these bugs are feeding on our sweat, why do we sweat at all?

Sweat is a major part of the body's temperature-control system. One function of your skin is to insulate your body, and stop it from getting too hot or cold. But it also uses special structures –

like hairs and sweat glands – to control your temperature when things get a little extreme.

When your body temperature drops – such as when you're caught outside in cold weather without a jacket – hairs embedded in the skin stand up to trap a layer of warm air near the skin. This prevents heat loss from the body, keeping you warm and toasty inside. But when your body temperature rises – like when you're exercising or lounging on the beach under a blazing sun – you need to lose heat, not retain it. So sweat glands deep beneath the skin release droplets of water on to the surface through tiny tubes called *sweat ducts*. Once there, these wet droplets evaporate, taking some extra heat with them.

So sweaty skin *does* have a purpose. It helps cool your body down.

So why is it just sweaty *feet* that stink?

Well, there are a few other stinky areas I can think of ...

OK — sweaty feet and armpits, then. You know what I mean. People don't usually have stinky knees or foreheads, do they?

Good point. Well, there are a couple of reasons for that. The first is that there are two different types of sweat gland in the body – called *eccrine* and *apocrine* glands. Eccrine sweat glands are found all over the body, from the scalp to the soles of the feet. They release a clear, watery kind of sweat to help regulate body temperature. Apocrine glands are found only in your armpits and – ahem – nether regions. They produce a thick, milky, yellowish sweat rich in proteins and fats – partly to expel waste chemicals from the body, and partly to communicate your own particular odour to other people. (Other animals use these smells to attract partners, but biologists are still arguing about whether this works the same way in humans!)

Unfortunately, the rich, milky apocrine-gland sweat from your armpits is also particularly tasty to bacteria, which helpfully munch on your proteins and release stinky chemicals as waste (i.e. stinky sweat = bug farts). *This* explains why armpit sweat smells different from, say, forehead sweat. And it also explains why we tend to apply deodorants (chemicals that mask or absorb stinky sweat smells) to our armpits, but not our foreheads.

That still doesn't explain why *feet* stink . . .

You're right, it doesn't. Or why some people's feet are stinkier than others. The simple answer to that one is this: some people sweat more than others (adults and teenagers, for example, sweat more than children), and some people – frankly – wash their socks more than others.

While the eccrine-gland sweat released from your feet isn't particularly tasty to bacteria, if there's enough of it the bugs will still bring the party to your trainers. If several days' worth of foot-sweat is trapped in the warm, cosy confines of an unwashed pair of socks or trainers, then the bacteria build up, and their stinky, cheese-smelling waste products build up along with them. And since some people sweat more than others, some people – and I'm not saying it's you, necessarily – should change their socks more often. At least, if they want to avoid being called Captain Reekyfeet . . .

Get it sorted: sweaty stuff

* The average adult has almost *3 million* sweat glands, which are found more or less everywhere on the body except for the lips and nipples.
* In a tropical climate, you can sweat 2-3 litres of water every hour!
* Sufferers of the disease *Chromohidrosis* have malfunctioning sweat glands which produce multicoloured sweat, in shades including red, blue, green, yellow and black.

Why don't snakes blink?

Because they don't have eyelids! Or rather, they don't have *movable* eyelids. Instead, they have transparent scales over each eye. These protect their eyes like a pair of goggles.

Snakes wear goggles?

In a manner of speaking, yes. Although unlike us, they can't take their goggles off.

Weird. Does that mean they can swim?

Well, yes. As a matter of fact, almost all snakes can swim. (Most of them can climb too. So if you're ever trying to escape from one in the jungle, don't dive into a river or climb a tree!) But that isn't really why they evolved their scaly goggles. Or why they lost their eyelids in the first place.

Wait — so snakes *had* eyelids once? Now I'm really confused . . .

Don't be. It's simple, really. Look at it this way – what are eyelids for?

Errr, I dunno. Keeping your eyes clean? Helping you sleep?

Partly, yes.* Eyelids protect eyeballs, keeping them

---

* Although you don't need to close your eyes to sleep. Many animals with eyelids – including lions, tigers and wolves – are quite capable of sleeping with one or both eyes open. Even humans do it. Well,

moist and free of dirt, grime and harmful bacteria. Fish don't have eyelids (just picture the lifeless, doll-like stare of a shark), because they don't need them to keep their eyes moist and well washed underwater. But frogs, newts and salamanders do. Millions of years ago, when fish began emerging from the seas and evolving into amphibians, they found themselves in dirty, gritty air that could dry out their eyes and blind them, making it hard to hunt or avoid being hunted.

But a few mutant ones with extra flaps of skin above or below their eyes did a little better in the new, airy environment. These eye-flap mutants survived better than those with no eye-flaps at all, and over time these simple eye-flaps evolved into movable eyelids that could blink to clear dirt or stay closed to help keep the eye moist during sleep. After a while, some of those amphibians made their permanent home on the land and evolved into reptiles, like lizards, turtles and dinosaurs. Which therefore have (or had) eyelids too.

some of them, anyway. In fact, my brother sometimes falls asleep with his eyes open. Which freaks everybody out, but has never done him any harm.

Hang on a minute — aren't snakes reptiles too?

Well spotted. Yes, they are. Snakes are ancient reptiles of the serpent family.[*] They evolved from a single group of legless burrowing lizards which do have eyelids. But somewhere along the way, they lost them.

But why?

No one knows for sure. But many biologists think it was to make them better burrowers and hunters. Instead of closing their eyes to protect them from dirt as they burrowed – or slithered after prey through thick undergrowth – snakes evolved a permanent, see-through scale over each eye. These transparent scales – called *brilles* – allowed snakes to burrow and slither with their eyes wide open, making it easier for them to find and chase prey. And once they had evolved these handy dirt-goggles, there was little point in having eyelids any more. (Think about it – you don't need to close your eyes underwater when you're wearing goggles in the pool, do you?) So eventually, they lost their eyelids entirely.

So do these goggle-wearing snakes have good eyesight, then?

Some do. Tree snakes, for example, have very

---

[*] Or technically, the sub-order *Serpentes*. Latin always sounds more posh and impressive to your mates at the zoo.

good eyesight, and use it to spot prey among leafy treetops. But most burrowing snakes have pretty poor vision. And – lacking external ears of any kind – they're also completely deaf. It seems that snakes have become so good at hunting things in burrows and thick undergrowth that they no longer need their eyes or ears much to do it.

But how can they hunt if they can't see or hear anything?

Most snakes use their incredibly keen senses of touch, taste and smell to track and capture prey. While they don't have ears, their bodies and jawbones are very sensitive to vibrations coming through the ground. So they can track a scampering mouse by 'listening' for its footsteps in the earth. Some snakes – like pit vipers – can also detect an animal's body heat, using infrared sense organs behind their nostrils. In this way, they can 'see' the warm outline of a mouse's body against the cooler background of plants and rocks. A bit like those cool infrared goggles soldiers use.

So they don't just have goggles, they have night-vision goggles? Man — snakes are *cool*!

Yup. But perhaps their most important senses are the combined supersense of taste and smell. When a snake flicks its tongue out, it's actually smelling and tasting the air. The tongue samples the air and passes it to a special organ in the roof of the mouth, called the Jacobsen's organ, which is so sensitive that a snake can taste week-old footprints in the ground, or sniff out water particles from rivers hundreds of metres away. With this, the snake builds up a kind of smell-a-vision picture of the world around it, navigating and hunting by smell and taste alone. Which can be a big advantage on a dark night.

So snakes are basically deadly ninja mouse-assassins.

Errr, well, they eat insects, frogs, birds and mammals too. But in a way, yes.

Coooooooool-ness. OK — one more question. If a snake doesn't have eyelids, how can you tell if he's asleep?

Good question. It's not easy.

One way is to watch for the tongue. If the tongue is flicking out once in a while, the snake is probably awake. If there's no tongue-flicking at all for several minutes, it's probably asleep. But then again, I wouldn't count on it . . .

Snake stuff:
top 10 facts about serpents

1 Snakes are very ancient – they've been around for over 150 million years.
2 A human backbone contains 33 bones (or *vertebrae*). Snakes have up to 400.
3 Except for sea snakes, snake skins are actually dry and smooth rather than wet and slimy.
4 Pet snakes can live in captivity for over forty years.
5 Snakes are found on every continent except Antarctica.
6 There are no wild snakes in Ireland or New Zealand.
7 Most snakes are not venomous, but a few are *seriously* venomous and can kill a healthy adult human with a single bite.
8 King cobras generally avoid humans. But if cornered, they can deliver enough venom in a single bite to kill twenty people.
9 Green Anacondas can weigh up to 250kg – more than most Grizzly Bears.
10 Black Mambas are among the fastest snakes in the world. They can slither at over 12mph (20km/h). The fastest human in the world – sprinter Usain Bolt – can hit 23mph (37km/h). So while he might be fine, the rest of us had better steer clear of angry mambas!

Why does your tummy rumble when you're hungry?

Because when your brain senses that you're hungry, it empties your stomach, squeezing out stomach gases and half-digested slop to make room for the lovely grub to come. As these gases and liquids gurgle through your guts, they create loud rumbling noises in your belly.

Really? Like gurgling drainpipes inside your body?

Exactly. Only the pipes are meaty and have more twists and turns. And they're filled with half-digested liquid food (called *chyme*) rather than rainwater.

Hmmm. It doesn't sound much like a gurgle in *my* belly. More like a growling bear or something.

That's because the sound changes as it vibrates through the muscle, meaty fibres and skin of your belly, so that by the time it gets to the outside, the sound is much lower-pitched. Technically, tummy rumbles are called *borborgymi*.* And you're right – by the time they get to the outside, they sound more like low growls than tinkly

---

* And if you say 'borborgymi' in a silly, low-pitched voice, it sounds like just like the thing it describes!

gurgles. But if you put your ear to someone's belly just as it rumbles,* you'll hear the high gurgly bit beneath the rumble, which you can't normally hear from a distance.

But why would you want your stomach to squeeze shut if you're about to eat something? Wouldn't you want it to stay open, so you can digest things?

It doesn't really squeeze shut. It just contracts a bit to push out the stuff that's still in there, in order to make room for more. And in fact, not much digestion goes on in the stomach at all.

Eh? I thought the stomach had acids in it that melt and digest your food for you . . .

Well, it does contain acids that break the food down a bit. And together with the churning, mashing muscles of the stomach wall, these help liquefy your food. This is partly to make digestion easier later on, but mostly so you can fit more grub in your stomach at once. The main function of the stomach is to receive mashed-up food blobs from the mouth and hold them in storage for a bit, before they're passed through the gut for digestion.

The stomach doesn't extract the nutrients from your food – that's the job of the intestines.

---

* Make sure you ask permission – or at least warn the person – before you do this. Otherwise you'll get some very strange looks.

The stomach is basically a big, fat holding bag in your digestive system that allows you to eat large amounts of food at once, instead of slowly grazing away all day. It evolved so that we (and other animals) can 'eat and run' – snarfing large quantities of food on the move, and keeping them in store for slow digestion later on.

OK . . . so how does your brain know you're hungry in the first place?

Basically, it senses changes in the levels of sugars and fats in your bloodstream. When levels drop too low, the brain releases clever chemical messengers (called hormones) into your blood that make you feel hungry and want to seek out food. Then, when you finally find food, it sends quicker signals (through nerves) to your mouth, stomach and gut, preparing them for fast and efficient grub intake. Often, even *looking* at food can be enough to trigger these nerve signals.

Is that why we sometimes drool and slobber when we see tasty-looking foods?

Yep. These brain-body (or *psychosomatic*) signals were discovered by a famous Russian biologist and psychologist named Ivan Pavlov. He revealed them by ringing a bell every time he fed a group of dogs. After a while, the dogs would drool at the sound of the bell alone, proving that it wasn't the food itself that was making the dogs

slobber – it was the thought of food (or rather, hearing something that made them think of food, even if the food wasn't present).

In the same way, when you haven't eaten for a while, and you're suddenly presented with a steak, cake or milkshake, you'll start to drool from salivary glands under your tongue and at the back of your mouth. As you munch and chew, the saliva starts to break down starchy bits of your food, and keeps it moist so that it slides down your food-tube (or oesophagus) more easily.

Wow. I'm getting hungry just thinking about it, now . . .

If you like, you can go even further, and do a little brain-body experiment. Try this:

Imagine you're lost in a hot, dry desert and you haven't eaten for days.

Now picture, in your mind, a huge, fat, juicy hamburger. Really see it in your mind's eye, every detail – the rich, luscious meat . . . the crunchy lettuce beneath . . . the tomato, both sweet and sour, on top . . .

Now imagine raising the burger to your open mouth . . . the smell of it wafting up your nostrils as you take a big, juicy bite . . .

Drooling yet?

Ohhhhhhhhhhhhhhh. No fair. That does it – I'm off to McDonald's . . .

Have fun!

Why do your fingers go wrinkly in the bath?

Because your skin is actually an organ system made up of separate layers of tissue. Spend too long in the bath, and the dry, outer layer will expand and spread out, while the layer beneath stays put. This creates folds and wrinkles in spots where your skin is especially tight – like your feet, hands and fingertips.

Wait – skin is an organ?

Yes, it is. In fact, it's the largest organ in the body.

But I thought organs were, y'know, like big lumps of meaty stuff . . .

Well, an organ is just a collection of tissues that work together for a common purpose. And while most organs are a bit easier to play football with, that doesn't mean your skin doesn't qualify. Skin isn't just a flat, boring sheet of body tissue. It's actually very complex. It's made up of two main tissue layers – called the *dermis* and *epidermis* – and also contains other tissues like hair, nails, glands and nerve endings. Skin varies in thickness from 2 to 4mm – thinner in some places (like the knees and elbows) and thicker in others (like the soles of the feet).

The *dermis* (which is Latin for 'skin') is a rich

living layer of skin cells, blood vessels, sweat glands and oil glands. This is the pink, bloody bit that gets exposed if you manage to graze or chop off more than a few millimetres of skin in an accident. But ordinarily you never see it, as above (or outside) this lies the epidermis.

The *epidermis* (which means 'outer skin') itself contains four layers – an outer layer of hard, dry, dead skin cells that are constantly shed from the body, and three underlying layers of living skin cells that grow, divide and push upwards to replace the ones you've shed.

It's the *outer* part of the epidermis that goes wrinkly in the bath. This is because, while the cells in the under-layer are firmly attached to each other, and to the dermis beneath, the cells in the outer layer are not. So when your warm bath water is absorbed into the dry outer layer of the epidermis, it swells up, spreads out and forms ripples and wrinkles. This is mostly due to a skin protein called keratin, which helps to keep the tough, outer layer of skin waterproof. When it's dry, keratin forms wide flat sheets. But when it absorbs water, the protein twists and folds in on itself, creating wrinkles in the sheets.

But why doesn't that happen all the time — like every time you wash your hands?

Because ordinarily your epidermis is kept oily and waterproof by proteins and oil glands in the dermis. But if you spend too long underwater (and especially in warm water), the oil gets washed out, and water begins to seep in. The longer you stay in the bath, the more water is absorbed, and the wrinklier you get.

So if you stayed in there long enough, would you end up looking like an old granny? Or a big pink raisin?

Thankfully, no. There's only so much water your skin can absorb, so there a limit to how wrinkly you can get.

That's a relief. So is that what skin is for, then? To keep water out?

Actually, it's designed to keep water in, rather than out. Since your body is 60–75% water, it has to keep as much of it in as possible – only allowing out small amounts through sweat, tears and urine. So the tough, oily barrier of your skin helps prevent your body from dehydrating. And as an organ system, skin does loads of other useful jobs within the body.

Like what?

Well, it's not just a barrier to water. It also forms a fleshy shield against bacteria, viruses and other nasty microbes. It protects our bodies from harmful chemicals and radiation. It stores fat and water, which help to insulate the body against extreme temperatures, and it helps to control our inner body temperature, using hairs and sweat glands to trap and release heat.

Wow! Skin is pretty clever stuff.

That's not all! Skin is also a huge sense organ, and without it you'd have serious trouble figuring out what the world around you was up to. Nerve endings embedded in your skin sense temperature, pressure and pain, and they work together to give you your sense of touch. Without it, you'd have serious trouble walking and picking things up, let alone running, dancing, writing, drawing, or playing video games. And believe it or not, skin even helps with digestion and nutrition.

What!? How?

For starters, your skin uses sunlight to produce vitamin D, which helps you to absorb nutrients, such as calcium. The skin helps you get rid of things too. While body wastes and toxic chemicals are mostly peed and pooed out of your body, they're also sweated out through your skin. Your skin can even absorb some medicines that help to keep you healthy. Ever seen those medicine 'patches' people slap on their arm? Well, it's through capillaries (tiny blood vessels) in the skin that these drugs and medicines are taken into the bloodstream. In the future, more and more of our medicines might be delivered this way, rather than in pills and injections.

But you can't actually *eat* through your skin, right?

Right. Sadly, most food particles are too large to get through. And even if you could absorb food through your skin, your immune cells would probably just attack the undigested food blobs once they made it into your bloodstream, thinking they were dangerous bacteria. So while slapping beef stew on like suntan lotion might be fun, it won't do you much good.

It might, however, make you very popular with your dog . . .

Why do cats hide their claws but dogs don't?

Because dogs *can't* retract their claws – even if they want to – as their paws and claws are built differently from those of cats. And for good reason. While dogs basically only need blunt claws for digging, cats need sharp, retractable claws to stalk, thrive and survive.

Wait — so dogs can't actually retract their claws at all? Not even a bit?

Nope. Their doggy paws just aren't built for it. Like most other mammals, cats and dogs have 'finger' bones within their paws, called *phalanges*. Each claw-tipped 'toe' on the paw contains three phalange bones. We humans have phalanges too, in our hands and feet. If you look at your own hand, with your fingers outstretched, the phalanges are the bones that lie between your knuckles and finger joints. You have three phalanges in each finger (except for the thumb, in which the middle phalange bone is missing). Same goes for the feet. There are three phalanges in each toe (although they can be harder to spot compared with the ones in the fingers).

OK . . . so what makes a cat's phalanges different?

In humans, gorillas, dogs and most other mammals, the three phalanges are very similar to each other in shape (they just get a little smaller and thinner as they get closer to the tip of the finger or toe). But in cats, the final 'toe-tip' phalange – the one with the claw attached – is a different shape to all the others, and is attached to the phalange behind it by three or four special fleshy bands or *ligaments*. (For us, it would feel a bit like having four elastic bands looped between our knuckles, only the bands would be less stretchy.)

When the cat's paw is relaxed (with its toes curled under, like a loose fist), the ligaments above the phalanges remain short and tight, holding the claw up and back. But when the cat's paw is flexed (with its toes held out straight, like the fingers of a flat, open hand), the ligaments below the

phalanges tug on the base of the final 'toe-tip', levering the claw forward and down. So when it wants to use its claws to scratch, the cat extends and spreads the 'fingers and toes' on each paw. As soon as it relaxes and folds them again, the claws retract. This helps cats keep their claws sharp when they're not in use, preventing them from being ground down with each padding footstep, as dogs' claws are.

But wouldn't having sharper claws help dogs too? Like, make them better at hunting and defending themselves?

Not really, no. Because cats and dogs hunt (and fight) in very different ways. When hunting, dogs (and related species like wolves, hyenas and dingoes) tend to work in packs, chasing down their prey at a steady run. When their prey becomes too exhausted to escape or fight back, they move in for the kill with snapping jaws and teeth. Blunt claws give dogs grip while running and help them to dig and bury any bits of meat or bone they want to save for later. But sharp claws wouldn't do these jobs any better.

Cats, on the other hand, tend to hunt alone. And in general,* they prefer the stealthy, stalk-

---

* There are, of course, a few exceptions to this. Lionesses hunt in packs, and cheetahs are partial to high-speed chases. But most cats really can't be bothered with that kind of thing. And even lionesses and cheetahs sneak as close as possible to their prey before they unleash the final charge.

and-pounce method to a lengthy chase. Feline hunters like to approach their prey quietly, getting as close as possible before they make their move. Then they spring forward with claws outstretched, tripping up their prey and pinning them to the ground, and finish 'em off with a swift and deadly bite to the neck.

So you see now why cats need to be able to retract their claws. On the sneaky, stalking approach, keeping the claws inside their soft, padded paws helps muffle their footsteps, and prevents the clicking or scrabbling noises their claws would otherwise make. Then, when they pounce, claws kept sharp inside their fuzzy feet help them to snag and hold down struggling prey. Plus, of course, they make very handy weapons in a cat-scrap. Corner an angry kitty (or, for that matter, lion, tiger or leopard), and you'll soon see the claws come out.

Is that it, then? Cats hide their claws to keep them quiet, and to keep them sharp for attacking?

Well, there's one more reason why cats like to keep their claws sharp. *Climbing*. While very few dogs* can climb at all, almost *all* cats are good climbers. Some – like leopards and jaguars – are *phenomenal* climbers. They

---

* Some, like the Singing Dogs of New Guinea, can and do climb trees. But they're a rare exception to the general, doggy rule.

practically *run* up trees, rather than claw their way up them. Leopards even drag their kill up into trees to protect it from non-climbing scavengers like wild hunting dogs and hyenas. Wild dogs and wolf packs make formidable fighters and foragers. But when it comes down to agile hunting and deadly attacking . . . you can't beat a silent, sneaky cat.

So dogs are like tough, hard-nut hunting gangs, while cats are like ninja assassins — who strike without warning and slip away into the night . . .

Something like that, yes.

Coooool. I wish I was a ninja-cat assassin. You know what? That would make a great video game . . .

What?

Think about it — *Ninja Cat Assassin 3D*! You could stalk rats and mice, annoy the dog, trip people up on the stairs — it'd be brilliant!

Errr . . . OK . . . if you say so.

I'm calling the PlayStation people right now . . .

Facts about cats

* There are over 500 million domestic cats in the world, with 33 officially recognized breeds.
* Calico (or tortoiseshell) cats are almost always female.
* The average life expectancy for a house cat is 15 years; for a stray cat, only 3–5 years.
* Unlike dogs, cats *can* see colours, but they have trouble telling reds and greens apart.
* It's true that cats always land on their feet. Or at least, they do if they're given time to adjust in mid-air. As they fall, they do a special acrobatic twisting sequence – first the head turns towards the ground, then the upper body and front legs, and finally the back legs. With all this done, they round their back and extend their feet to lessen the impact on landing.

Those clever ninja kitties.

Why do leaves fall off trees in the autumn?

Some – but not all – trees drop their leaves in the autumn to prepare for the harsh winter to come. Dropping leaves helps some plants to save energy and water and also helps prevent them from freezing to death in low temperatures.

So trees drop their leaves on purpose?

Some do, yes.

That doesn't make sense.

Why not?

Well, how does lopping off leaves help a plant save energy? Don't plants need leaves to grow?

That's right, they do. As you've probably learned in biology at school, plant leaves are a bit like living solar panels. They use energy from sunlight to turn water and carbon-dioxide gas into sugars,* in a process called *photosynthesis*. These energy-rich plant sugars then feed their own growth – along with that of all the animals that eat the seeds, fruit or body of the plant.

---

* Plus, luckily for us, a bit of oxygen on the side. Without plants and photosynthesis, we air-breathing animals would have no air to breathe.

Yeah, I know all that. But doesn't losing leaves mean fewer solar panels, less energy and less growth for the plant? That's like chopping your fingers off to save supplying them with blood. You might save a bit of energy, but now you've got no fingers, you can't pick up any more food.

Well, yes – losing leaves does mean less growth. But sometimes that's not such a bad thing. Growing and maintaining leaves, seeds and fruit requires energy and water. Plants receive and trap their energy from sunlight and get water and nutrients from the soil around their roots. But in a harsh winter, sunlight, soil nutrients and free water in the soil all become more scarce. So if, in these tough winter conditions, the plant recklessly spends all its energy growing, seeding and fruiting, it might not survive long.

So it's less like

chopping off fingers and more like going into hibernation. In wintry climes, many animals – like squirrels, bats, bears and badgers – hibernate through the harsh winter. Rather than use up lots of energy staying warm and hunting during the coldest, leanest months, they feed up in the autumn, then sleep deeply to save energy right through the winter. Then in spring, when food becomes more plentiful, they emerge to start feeding and thriving again. When trees and plants drop their leaves in winter, they're doing much the same thing.

I s'pose that makes sense, now you put it that way. But how does dropping leaves help prevent trees from freezing? Wouldn't they stay warmer with more layers on, like winter coats on furry animals?

You might think so, yes. But again – you can't really compare the leaves of a plant with the furry coat of an animal. Fur evolved to trap warm air near the skin of mammals, keeping them toasty in cold weather. But leaves don't really serve that purpose. Leaves are basically for *trapping sunlight*, and for *exchanging gases and water*. Each leaf contains hundreds of little pores or gaps called *stomata*. The plant opens and closes these to control how much carbon dioxide comes into the leaf, and how much oxygen and water vapour are let out. In summer, this all ticks along nicely.

But in winter, the watery leaves can freeze solid, drawing heat from the body of the plant itself. And while many plants contain clever 'antifreeze' chemicals to prevent their cells being damaged by freezing, it's a much safer tactic to simply drop your watery leaves before the winter to prevent heat loss. Dropping leaves also protects some trees from becoming weighed down with heavy snowfall, which can topple the tree, damaging its trunk and roots. So there are lots of reasons to do it!

Hmmmm. OK — I get that. But there's one more thing I've never sussed out . . .

What's that?

Why do the leaves on some trees change colour before they drop off? Is it some sort of signal to the other trees, so they all know to do it at once?

No, not quite. Trees can't see each other, and – as far as we know – don't signal each other to drop their leaves. Instead, the leaf-drop (or *senescence*, as biologists call it) is usually triggered when the tree senses (using special shape-shifting proteins within the leaves) a drop in the number of daylight hours, or by a drop in temperatures below a certain level.

The reason the leaf changes colour is because of the light-trapping proteins, or *pigments*, within the leaf. These are the same proteins that help trap energy from sunlight during photosynthesis. The main pigment is called *chlorophyll*, and it absorbs the blue and red bits from sunlight while reflecting most of the green (which is why leaves look green in the first place).

Now sometimes there are also reddish, yellowish and orangey pigments within the leaf – chemicals that absorb and reflect different bits of sunlight. But there's so much more of the chlorophyll that you can't see them. *Except*, that is, when the leaf-drop (or senescence) is triggered. When that happens, the green chlorophyll pigment breaks down first, leaving the red, yellow or orange pigments behind. Eventually, these break down too, and the leaf goes brown and falls off. But for a few days or weeks, the autumn leaves seem to burst into flame as bright red, orange and yellow leaves appear all over the place.

Who knows – on some other planet, somewhere out in Space, there might be trees with blue or purple pigments instead. Then maybe there would be bright blue tropical rainforests, and beaches lined with purple palm trees.

Wow! I'd love to see that!

Me too . . .

Do bugs have bottoms?

Yes, they do. Albeit very small, bug-sized ones. All but the very oldest and simplest animal species have bottoms. As far as Mother Nature is concerned, if you have a mouth, you need a bottom. Any other arrangement would be a recipe for disaster.

Disaster? Why?

Well, think about it – what are mouths and bottoms actually for?

Eating food. And . . . err . . . getting rid of it.

Exactly.

So if you were an animal with a mouth but no bottom, would you, like, swell up and explode or something?

Sort of, yes. Keep cramming food into a tube with only one open end, and eventually the food will either spill back out of the top, or the tube itself will split apart. Once food and water has passed your stomach, fleshy valves prevent it moving back in there from the guts (or intestines) further down. So without an 'exit' for your digested food and body wastes, poo would pile up in your intestine until the gut wall burst or split – or you vomited it back up (and, yes, that does happen!) – allowing the bacteria from your gut to infect and poison your insides.

Ouch!

So, you see, bottoms are rather important. Which is why almost all animals – including bugs – have them.

Almost all? So a few animals *don't* have mouths or bottoms?

Right. While the vast majority of animal species do have separate mouths, bottoms and food-tubes, the simplest and most ancient animal families on the planet do not. These include sponges, starfish, jellyfish and anemones. Some of these animals have no mouth and bottom at all. Others lack a *separate* mouth and bottom.

Eh? What does that mean?

It means they have their mouth and bottom in the same place – using the same, single . . . ahem . . . opening for both purposes. So I guess you could say they have a *bouth*. Or a *mottom*.

Yuck! Gross!

You asked.

Buy why is it only the *oldest* animal types that have no proper bottom?

Because – just like eyes, arms, legs and everything else – mouths, bottoms and digestive systems have *evolved* in the animal kingdom. Before the animals came bacteria and other tiny, single-celled creatures like amoebas.* When you're only one cell wide, it's simple enough to absorb nutrients from the water or air around you and immediately put them to use inside your body. This is called intracellular (or 'inside-cell') digestion, and all single-celled life forms do it.

But if you've evolved into something a bit more complex – a multi-celled animal like a sponge, flatworm, fish or ferret – then things are a little different. Now you're going to need ways of getting nutrients from the outside of your body to the bits deeper inside – to the hungry organs buried beneath layer upon layer of body cells and tissues.

Sponges – the simplest multi-celled animals – get around this with lots of little channels or cavities in their bodies, which allow tiny nutrient

---

* Actually the correct word for more than one amoeba is *amoebae*. Which, when correctly pronounced, rhymes with 'Phoebe'. This makes me wonder what would be the correct name for a group of girls all called Phoebe . . .

molecules from the water around them to pass deep into their bodies. Once inside these *digestive cavities*, the nutrients are absorbed and digested inside the cells, much as they are in bacteria.

So do jellyfish and starfish have these cavities too?

Jellyfish, starfish and anemones go one better. Since they have to eat larger food morsels (like plankton, crabs and small fish) they have a *digestive duffle*. This is a big fleshy bag inside their bodies, within which their prey is broken down by acids and digestive juices. This done, they absorb the nutrients and allow the rest to fall out, along with any other wastes from their bodies. So the opening to the digestive duffle – usually surrounded by arms or tentacles – works as both a mouth *and* a bottom. And you could say it either has both, or neither.

Ahh — now I get it. So what was the first animal with a mouth *and* a bottom? You know, in two different places. Separate, like.

That would have been something like a flatworm. Active, complex animals like worms, crustaceans and insects were the first animals on the planet to evolve a food-tube – otherwise known as a *digestive tract*. In worms, this tract is just a simple tube running from an opening at the head end (the mouth) to an exit at the back (the bottom*).

In prawns, lobsters and crayfish, it's the tube that runs along the back of the animal, where you'd expect the spine to be. This is often mistaken for a blood vessel or 'vein', and when chefs chop them out to make seafood taste better, they say the prawn or shrimp has been 'de-veined'. They're quite wrong, of course. It's not a vein at all – it's the digestive tract, filled with fishy-smelling prawn poo. Like all invertebrates, these animals have no backbones, and their guts run down their back (or dorsal) side.

In vertebrates (animals with backbones), the digestive tract runs along the belly, rather than the back. Newts, frogs, cats, dogs, hippos, horses, humans and other vertebrates have food-tubes that are up to ten times longer than their bodies, coiled up inside to save space. These super-long guts give more surface area for absorbing nutrients, and have specialized pouches and organs for storing food and making digestive juices. This allows vertebrates to eat larger chunks of food at once, to digest tougher food sources and to survive for longer periods without eating.

So worms, prawns, bugs, snakes, spiders and frogs all have bottoms too?

Correct.

---

* Or as biologists call it, the *anus*. Which comes from the Latin word for 'ring'.

One more question, then —

What's that?

What does bug poo *look* like?

Well, a bit like ours. Only *much* smaller . . .

Gut stuff: facts about digestion

* The largest digestive tract on Earth belongs to the Blue Whale. An adult Blue Whale's gut can be up to 250m (830 feet) long, and is wide enough for a child to swim through.
* Hyenas have among the most powerful digestive systems of all animals, which allows them to scavenge body parts that other animals cannot eat. Their powerful jaws help them pulverize and swallow and digest the hardest bone. Only teeth, hair and horns are brought back up, undigested.
* In snails and other molluscs, the digestive tract is twisted around inside the shell, leaving their bottoms situated above their heads.

Why is the sky blue?

Simple, really. Because the sky is just loads of air stuck to the planet, and air is not see-through – it's blue.

Eh? Wait a minute — I thought air was invisible . . .

Ah, there's the thing, see. Small amounts of air *are* pretty much clear or transparent (and just very, very slightly bluish). So it *seems* like air is invisible. But if you get a big chunk of air in one place and try to look through it, you see that all that 'slightly bluish' adds up to a very real and obvious blue colour. And that's what we see in the sky: a massive layer of air, made of billions and billions of very slightly blue air molecules, giving us a beautiful sky-blue . . . er . . . sky.

Is that it, then? The sky is blue because air is a bit blue?!

Pretty much. Same thing goes for the water in lakes and oceans: they look blue because water isn't colourless either – it's very slightly blue. Look down through thousands of tonnes of it and it looks blue, but scoop out a glass of it and it looks clear. That's why the thin layer of seawater that washes on to the beach with each wave is clear, but the ocean itself is blue.

But I heard the sea is blue because it's reflecting the sky . . .

Sorry – lots of people (including some teachers!) say this, but it simply isn't true. Think about it: haven't you ever seen a blue sea under a cloudy white or grey sky? Exactly. The sea might not look as *bright* a blue colour on cloudy days, because less light is getting through the clouds to shine into and off the water. But it's still blue, rather than pure grey or white.

But that's simple!

Yes, it is. Of course, if you want to know why *air* is blue in the first place, then things could get really interesting . . .

Go on, then.

People often use the words 'air' and 'oxygen' as if they mean the same thing. But while there is plenty of oxygen in air, what we call 'air' is actually lots of different gases mixed together. This includes some weird exotic ones like xenon and argon, but it's mostly made of nitrogen (about 78%) and oxygen (about 21%). Anyway – when light from the Sun hits these gas molecules, some of the light goes straight through them, and some of it gets absorbed by the molecules and thrown back out again. Now here's the tricky bit: the light from the Sun is white, but white light actually contains all the colours of the rainbow –

something scientists call the *spectrum* of visible light. (Isaac Newton showed us that a few hundred years ago by using glass shapes to split it up.)

OK ...

Colours all look different to us because they all have different *frequencies*. Don't worry about what *frequency* means for now – it's enough to know that the blue-green end of the light spectrum has a higher frequency than the red-orange end. So yellow light has a higher frequency than red light, green is higher than yellow, blue is higher than green, and so on.

Erm ... my brain hurts ...

Stick with it – we're nearly there. Now, remember those gas molecules in the air? Well, they tend to absorb and scatter only the high-frequency (or the green and blue) bits of the light that hit them; the low-frequency (red and orange) bits go straight through. So as light from the Sun comes through the air in the Earth's atmosphere, the blue bits of it get scattered a lot more than the red bits. These blue bits get scattered all over the sky so seem to come from everywhere when we look up at it. Hence, the big blue sky.

Got it. But what about sunsets? Then the sky looks red ...

At sunset (and sunrise too), the Sun is low on the horizon. When this happens, the light from it has to cut diagonally through the atmosphere (instead of straight down and through, as it does when the Sun is right overhead). This means the light has to come through more air than usual before making it to our eyes. More air means more scattering – and even the red bits get lobbed about this time. So before the Sun's rays are hidden from us at sunset, and just as they start to appear at sunrise, we're treated to a fiery skyful of scattered red light.

Why is snot green?

Basically, because it's the result of a fight between nasty bugs and body cells that make a green-coloured goo.

What?!

Seriously. Snot is made of a sticky substance produced inside the nose that traps and flushes out harmful bacteria. These nasty bugs try to get up your nose when you breathe them in. The sticky stuff stops them getting down your throat and into your lungs, and it also contains cells that your body produces to fight and kill the bugs. It's these that make the green goo. Sneezing and blowing your nose help to clear it all out.

Ugh. Fine. But what do they make the green goo for?

The body cells form part of the incredibly clever and complex defence system in your body. They make special proteins called *lysozymes*, which help them bust open, eat and digest the bacteria – a bit like the acid in your stomach. For this reason, we call the cells *phagocytes*, which is Latin for 'eaty-cells' (which you may prefer, but biologists use 'phagocytes' because it sounds more important and clever). It's one of these bacteria-busting proteins that has the green colour.

But why green, and not blue or purple?

This is purely because the protein contains a form of iron that reflects green light and absorbs all the other colours. Incidentally, you find a similar protein in wasabi, the type of horseradish you eat with Japanese sushi, which is why that's green too. Think about that next time you eat horseradish. Or a bogey.

I don't eat bogeys. I don't even pick my nose.

Of course you don't. No one does. No one rolls them up and flicks them, or sticks them under the desk either.

That's right. But if someone did ... why would the bogey change colour to dark green, brown or black?

That's because once it's out of its warm, moist home in your nose, the snot begins to dry up as water from it evaporates into the air. When this happens, the phagocytes die and the greenish proteins within them break up – removing the green colour from the bogey.

After this, bacteria in the air settle on to the bogey and start to eat it (waste not, want not, as my mum always says). They chew up all the bits of phagocyte, dead bacteria and skin cells found in the snot, until all that's left is a dried-up mass of brownish-black protein leftovers. And even that gets eaten eventually.

Hang on a minute – how did you know bogeys change colour if you never pick your nose?

Oops.

Top 10 places to stick a bogey

1   Under a table
2   Under your chair
3   Under your tongue
4   On the wall
5   On a friend
6   In someone's pencil case
7   In someone's lunch
8   Behind a steering wheel
9   Behind your head
10 Back up your nose again

Why do people from different countries look different from each other?

Actually, people from different countries look pretty much the same. The differences that do exist – like skin colour and eye shape – are due to where our ancestors lived, and how they spread out from Africa and across the world.

But people *do* look different. And it seems like the further away they live from each other, the more different they look, right?

Well – sometimes, I guess. It's true that Chinese and Korean people look more similar to each other than, say, Chinese and African people do. But it's not where people live that makes them different.

What d'you mean?

Imagine this. Let's say I lined three average-looking white kids up next to each other, like a police identity parade – an American, an Australian and a South African. Assuming I didn't let them talk, could you pick out which one was which?

Probably not.

Right. And they're from different continents.

But that's cheating. They could all look the same because their families all came from the same part of Europe.

OK. So maybe it's not where you live now, but *where your ancestors came from* that makes you look different. Those three guys might look the same because their ancestors were all average-looking white Europeans.

All right, then — why do white Europeans, Chinese people and Africans all look different from each other?

Ahh – now we're getting somewhere. Good question. The short answer is this: their ancestors all started out in Africa, looking like Africans. But as they split off into groups and travelled across the globe, the descendants of the Chinese and Europeans gradually changed in appearance as they adapted to their new homes.

I don't get it.

Well, the only real difference between white Europeans and black Africans is their skin colour. Years ago, average-looking white European scientists used to tell us that this was because Africans

started out perfectly white (like them), but were tanned black by the sun. But they had it completely the wrong way round – in fact, those very same scientists (or rather, their ancestors) started out with black skin and became pasty as they moved northwards out of their homeland in Africa. This, it turns out, is due to vitamins.

What, those things you eat to stay healthy?

Yes, kind of. Vitamins are things your body needs to stay healthy, and we usually get them through food (and, more recently, pills). But your body can also make some vitamins for itself. Your skin can make vitamin D, which is important for healthy bones and teeth, but it needs plenty of sunlight to do so. In sunny regions, black skin lets through just enough sunlight to make vitamin D while also blocking the parts of sunlight that cause skin cancer. But in less sunny areas further north (or south), black skin blocks too much sun to allow vitamin D to be made properly. So the black African ancestors of white Europeans got pastier as they moved out of Africa and settled further north.

So what about Chinese people and African people? Why do they look so different from each other?

Well, the ancestors of the Chinese and other

Asian people also became paler as they moved northwards (and eastwards) out of Africa, for the same reason. The only other notable difference between Africans, Europeans and Asians is the shape of their eyes and eyelids. Asians tend to have more almond-shaped eyes, and have an extra fold of skin (called an *epicanthal fold*) on their eyelids. It is thought that this narrowing and shielding of the eyes evolved to help protect the ancient settlers of Asia from the blinding effects of the snows and winds of the mountains and plains. Some of them then passed this trait on to their Inuit and American Indian descendants, who crossed the land bridge from Asia to America thousands of years ago.

Is that it? We're all the same?

Yes.

And the only reason people look different at all is because of a bit of weather and a vitamin?

Exactly.

Kind of makes you wonder why we didn't figure all that out sooner.

Yep. It certainly does.

How loud can you burp?

The loudest burp on record is around 105 decibels – louder than a motorbike or chainsaw, and loud enough to cause real pain to anyone close enough to it. But don't try these at home, as they could be dangerous!

Louder than a motorbike?! No way!

Yup. The world-record burp measured 104.9 decibels (decibels, or dB for short, are the units used to measure volume). And that was from over 2.5m away! Close up, the World Champion burper claims to be able to reach 118dB or more. The average motorbike roars away at around 90dB – a full twenty-eight units lower!

So who did it?

An English guy called Paul Hunn. He smashed the previous burping record in July 2004, and no one has topped it yet.

How could he burp so loud?

Well, like all sounds, burps are just waves of air pressure, and, if you make these waves big enough, any sound can become loud. To create a sound, an object – like a bell or guitar string – is made to vibrate back and forth very fast by striking it, plucking it or rubbing something against it. In turn, the object compresses the air molecules around it, making waves or vibrations that are carried through the air. When they reach your ears, these pressure waves vibrate your eardrums. From there, the vibrations are amplified by a set of little bones, picked up by a set of tiny hairs in your

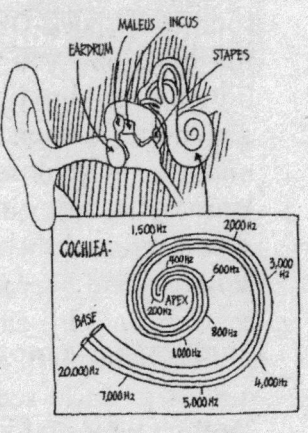

cochlea (which is a long, thin tube filled with fluid and lined with hairs – all coiled up like a snail shell in your inner ear). Here the vibrations are finally translated into nerve signals that your brain interprets as sounds, such as 'bell', 'guitar string' or whatever.

But what about burps?

In the case of burps, the vibrating object is a fleshy flap called the cardia, which closes off the stomach from the food-tube, or *oesophagus*. When air is swallowed (either by accident while you're eating, or on purpose if you're trying to force a burp), it gets trapped in the stomach. As the stomach fills with food, liquid and gas, the pressure builds up and the air bursts through the flap – vibrating it on the way out and creating that deep, satisfying BRRRRRRRRRRRRRRPPPPP sound as it goes. Of course, if you want to *force* the burp out, you can squeeze your stomach by contracting your stomach muscles and diaphragm (which is the flat sheet of muscle underneath your stomach and lungs). This is how Mr Hunn made his burp so loud. Millions of kids around the world use the same method to force loud burps. He's just much better at it than anyone else. Oh, and he also swallowed lots of fizzy drink first.

Yeah — why *do* fizzy drinks make you burp like that?

They're made bubbly and fizzy by adding carbon dioxide gas under pressure. So when you drink the drink, you swallow the gas. The gas builds up in your stomach, annnnd . . . you can figure out the rest.

Is it dangerous to make yourself burp like that?

Well, drinking lots of fizzy drinks isn't very good for you, and swallowing air on purpose won't do your stomach any good, but that's not really what makes burping as loud as Mr Hunn does dangerous. It's after the burp leaves the body that it becomes a danger to you and others.

But if a burp is just air and sound, how could it be dangerous to anyone?

If they're loud enough and at the right frequency, sounds can be very powerful and dangerous. Ever hear of opera singers who can shatter glass with their voices alone? Well, that's true. All they have to do is hit the right pitch, and sing the note loud enough, and the glass will vibrate and shake itself to pieces. And the US military have even developed a 'sound weapon' that fires waves of air pressure and sound instead of bullets. The Vortex Ring Gun shoots a ring of vibrating air that can knock down a grown man over 10m away.

So if you burped loud enough, could you crack a person's glasses? Or knock a bunch of people over? That'd be sweet!

Err ... no. Not quite. Even the most accomplished burper, like Mr Hunn, couldn't produce enough air pressure to knock someone down. And his burps are too low-pitched to crack glass. But he could burp loud enough to hurt your ears, or even damage them permanently.

What, really?

Yup – really. Mr Hunn burps at between 105 and 118 decibels. 85 decibels is enough to temporarily damage your hearing. Builders using pneumatic drills (which thump away at around 120dB) wear ear defenders to avoid getting hearing damage. If you burped at 165dB, that would be the same as a gunshot going off right next to your head. So burp this loud and you could deafen yourself and other people!

Yeah, and what a let-down too.

Why's that?

Just think — you can burp as loud as a gunshot, but after the first time no one can hear it. Not even you.

Err . . . yeah . . . that'd be a real tragedy.

Just one more thing . . .

What's that?

Do Brussels sprouts make you burp?

I don't . . . think so, no. Why do you ask?

They should do. Cos they come from Belch'um.

Oh *man*, that was bad.

Heh, heh. BUUUURRRRRRRRRRRPPPPP!!!!

Sci-facts: noisy stuff

The volume of a sound wave is related to its air pressure, and measured in decibels (dB). On the decibel scale, zero decibels marks the softest sound most people can hear (although some people can hear sounds at −10dB or lower). Here's how some common (and uncommon) noises measure up:

dB	Sound
0	rustling leaves
20	whisper
40	light rainfall
75	washing machine
90	motorbike
110	chainsaw, rock concert
115	one of Paul Hunn's burps (at close range)
130	jet aeroplane (from 30m away)
165	shotgun

More great books by
Glenn Murphy

Website Discount Offer

Get 3 for 2 on all Glenn Murphy books at www.panmacmillan.com

£1 postage and packaging costs to UK addresses, £2 for overseas

To buy the books with this special discount:

1.   visit our website, www.panmacmillan.com
2.   search by author or book title
3.   add to your shopping basket

Closing date is 31 July 2011.

Full terms and conditions can be found at www.panmacmillan.com

Registration is required to purchase books from the website.

The offer is subject to availability of stock and applies to paperback editions only.

≈ panmacmillan.com